FREE
THOUGHT
AND
OFFICIAL
PROPAGANDA

First Warbler Classics Edition 2024

"Free Thought and Official Propaganda" was a speech delivered at South Place Institute on March 24, 1922, as part of the Conway Memorial Lecture Series. The text was printed by Watts & Co., London, in 1922.

"Mysticism and Logic" was first published in the *Hibbert Journal* in July 1914.

Biographical Timeline © Warbler Press

ISBN 978-1-962572-76-7 (paperback)
ISBN 978-1-962572-77-4 (e-book)

www.warblerpress.com

FREE
THOUGHT
AND
OFFICIAL
PROPAGANDA

BERTRAND RUSSELL

warbler classics

CONTENTS

FREE THOUGHT AND
OFFICIAL PROPAGANDA

CHAIRMAN'S INTRODUCTORY ADDRESS[1]

I HAVE COME HERE to-night, partly because I want to hear Mr. Russell, and partly because of an old affection for South Place and its traditions. I myself have been for more than forty years a professional teacher; and it is as a teacher—who thirty-seven years ago was dismissed for refusing religious conformity—that I most easily approach the problem of free thought. Though systems of education professing to teach men and women how to think have been in use in Europe for, perhaps, three thousand years, we have not yet reached that degree of success which would be shown if most educated people came to much the same conclusions on the great problems of life from a study of the same evidence. Everywhere you have rebels; but ninety percent of French or American students of history come to French or American conclusions, and eighty-five percent of English students come to English conclusions; eighty percent of Eton boys hold Eton political opinions all their lives; ninety percent of the Irish Catholic population of the United States seem to hold generation after generation

---

1   The chairman was Graham Wallas (1858–1932), an English socialist, social psychologist, educationalist, a leader of the Fabian Society, and a co-founder of the London School of Economics.

identical opinions on religion and politics which are not held by the vast majority of Americans. It may be said that in these cases only one kind of evidence is allowed to reach the students in each institution. But everybody reads newspapers, and talks with his neighbours, and travels, and visits museums; and most intelligent people read books and magazines. Sooner or later much of the same evidence reaches us all. I myself believe that one of the main reasons why we do not to a greater degree draw the same conclusions from that evidence is that we do not really learn the difficult art of thought. A boy at school is taught to memorize and to understand mathematical formulæ or foreign languages or scientific statements. But in weighing evidence the effort of memorizing, and even the effort of understanding, are not of the first importance. The effective process is a sort of painful and watchful expectancy. A schoolboy or a college student finds that he has an uncomfortable sense of unreality in repeating some accustomed formula, or writing an essay to enforce some accustomed line of argument. He shrinks from that feeling, as all animals shrink from discomfort. If he were taught what are the conditions of effective thought, and were encouraged to act on that lesson, he would know that it is only by resolutely fastening on such vague and painful premonitions, and forcing them to come into full consciousness and disclose their deeper causes and tendencies that he can arrive at new truth or make some old truth his own.

But who is going to tell him this secret? Every day in London thousands of clever and sympathetic boys and girls begin the day by sitting through three-quarters of an hour of the dreary "Cowper-Temple" instruction which consists, as Bishop Temple once said, of teaching at everybody's expense what nobody believes. They may be conscious or half-conscious of a feeling of unreality; but, even if they have not been taught that it is a sacred duty to "struggle against doubt," they shrink, as the cleverest of them feel that the teacher is shrinking, from any further exploration on that path.

Perhaps someday the teachers and students of the ordinary school and college subjects may learn something from those little isolated institutions where men and women try to prepare themselves for the creative arts. The young painter or sculptor or member of a group of young poets is often queerly ignorant and one-sided. But he lives in another world from that of the big conventional sixth-form boy at Harrow or St. Paul's, or the hockey-playing athlete of a girls' High School, because he has felt the pain and the exhilaration reached through pain by which alone new truth and new beauty are born into the world.

FREE THOUGHT AND OFFICIAL PROPAGANDA

Moncure Conway, in whose honour we are assembled to-day, devoted his life to two great objects: freedom of thought and freedom of the individual. In regard to both these objects, something has been gained since his time, but something also has been lost. New dangers, somewhat different in form from those of past ages, threaten both kinds of freedom, and unless a vigorous and vigilant public opinion can be aroused in defence of them, there will be much less of both a hundred years hence than there is now. My purpose in this address is to emphasize the new dangers and to consider how they can be met.

Let us begin by trying to be clear as to what we mean by "free thought." This expression has two senses. In its narrower sense it means thought which does not accept the dogmas of traditional religion. In this sense a man is a "free thinker" if he is not a Christian or a Mussulman or a Buddhist or a Shintoist or a member of any of the other bodies of men who accept some inherited orthodoxy. In Christian countries a man is called a "free thinker" if he does not decidedly believe in God, though this would not suffice to make a man a "free thinker" in a Buddhist country.

I do not wish to minimize the importance of free thought

in this sense. I am myself a dissenter from all known religions, and I hope that every kind of religious belief will die out. I do not believe that, on the balance, religious belief has been a force for good. Although I am prepared to admit that in certain times and places it has had some good effects, I regard it as belonging to the infancy of human reason, and to a stage of development which we are now outgrowing.

But there is also a wider sense of "free thought," which I regard as of still greater importance. Indeed, the harm done by traditional religions seems chiefly traceable to the fact that they have prevented free thought in this wider sense. The wider sense is not so easy to define as the narrower, and it will be well to spend some little time in trying to arrive at its essence.

When we speak of anything as "free," our meaning is not definite unless we can say what it is free *from*. Whatever or whoever is "free" is not subject to some external compulsion, and to be precise we ought to say what this kind of compulsion is. Thus thought is "free" when it is free from certain kinds of outward control which are often present. Some of these kinds of control which must be absent if thought is to be "free" are obvious, but others are more subtle and elusive.

To begin with the most obvious. Thought is not "free" when legal penalties are incurred by the holding or not holding of certain opinions, or by giving expression to one's belief or lack of belief on certain matters. Very few countries in the world have as yet even this elementary kind of freedom. In England, under the Blasphemy Laws, it is illegal to express disbelief in the Christian religion, though in practice the law is not set in motion against the well-to-do. It is also illegal to teach what Christ taught on the subject of non-resistance. Therefore, whoever wishes to avoid becoming a criminal must profess to agree with Christ's teaching, but must avoid saying what that teaching was. In America no one can enter the country without first solemnly declaring that he disbelieves in anarchism and polygamy; and, once inside, he must also disbelieve in communism. In Japan it is illegal to express disbelief in the divinity of the Mikado. It will thus be seen that a voyage round the world is a perilous adventure. A Mohammedan, a Tolstoyan, a Bolshevik, or a Christian cannot undertake it without at some point becoming a criminal, or holding his tongue about what he considers important truths. This, of course, applies only to steerage passengers; saloon passengers are allowed to believe whatever they please, provided they avoid offensive obtrusiveness.

It is clear that the most elementary condition, if thought is to be free, is the absence of legal penalties for the expression of opinions. No great country has yet reached to this level, although most of them think they have. The opinions which are still persecuted strike the majority as so monstrous and immoral that the general principle of toleration cannot be held to apply to them. But this is exactly the same view as that which made possible the tortures of the Inquisition. There was a time when Protestantism seemed as wicked as Bolshevism seems now. Please do not infer from this remark that I am either a Protestant or a Bolshevik.

Legal penalties are, however, in the modern world, the least of the obstacles to freedom of thoughts. The two great obstacles are economic penalties and distortion of evidence. It is clear that thought is not free if the profession of certain opinions makes it impossible to earn a living. It is clear also that thought is not free if all the arguments on one side of a controversy are perpetually presented as attractively as possible, while the arguments on the other side can only be discovered by diligent search. Both these obstacles exist in every large country known to me, except China, which is the last refuge of freedom. It is these obstacles with which I shall be concerned—their present magnitude, the likelihood of their increase, and the possibility of their diminution.

We may say that thought is free when it is exposed to free competition among beliefs—i.e., when all beliefs are able to state their case, and no legal or pecuniary advantages or disadvantages attach to beliefs. This is an ideal which, for various reasons, can never be fully attained. But it is possible to approach very much nearer to it than we do at present.

Three incidents in my own life will serve to show how, in modern England, the scales are weighted in favour of Christianity. My reason for mentioning them is that many people do not at all realize the disadvantages to which avowed Agnosticism still exposes people.

The first incident belongs to a very early stage in my life. My father was a Freethinker, but died when I was only three years old. Wishing me to be brought up without superstition, he appointed two Freethinkers as my guardians. The Courts, however, set aside his will, and had me educated in the Christian faith. I am afraid the result was disappointing, but that was not the fault of the law. If he had directed that I should be educated as a Christadelphian or a Muggletonian or a Seventh-Day Adventist, the Courts would not have dreamed of objecting. A parent has a right to ordain that any imaginable superstition shall be instilled into his children after his death, but has not the right to say that they shall be kept free from superstition if possible.

The second incident occurred in the year 1910. I had at that time a desire to stand for Parliament as a Liberal, and the Whips recommended me to a certain constituency. I addressed the Liberal Association, who expressed themselves favourably, and my adoption seemed certain. But, on being questioned by a small inner caucus, I admitted that I was an Agnostic. They asked whether the fact would come out, and I said it probably would. They asked whether I should be willing to go to church occasionally, and I replied that I should not. Consequently, they selected another candidate, who was duly elected, has been in Parliament ever since, and is a member of the present Government.

The third incident occurred immediately afterwards. I was invited by Trinity College, Cambridge, to become a lecturer, but not a Fellow. The difference is not pecuniary; it is that a Fellow has a voice in the government of the College, and cannot be dispossessed during the term of his Fellowship except for grave immorality. The chief reason for not offering me a Fellowship was that the clerical party did not wish to add to the anti-clerical vote. The result was that they were able to dismiss me in 1916, when they disliked my views on the War.[2] If I had been dependent on my lectureship, I should have starved.

These three incidents illustrate different kinds of disadvantages attaching to avowed freethinking even in modern England. Any other avowed Freethinker could supply similar incidents from his personal experience, often of a far more serious character. The net result is that people who

---

2   I should add that they re-appointed me later, when war `passions had begun to cool.

are not well-to-do dare not be frank about their religious beliefs.

It is not, of course, only or even chiefly in regard to religion that there is lack of freedom. Belief in communism or free love handicaps a man much more than Agnosticism. Not only is it a disadvantage to hold those views, but it is very much more difficult to obtain publicity for the arguments in their favour. On the other hand, in Russia the advantages and disadvantages are exactly reversed: comfort and power are achieved by professing Atheism, communism, and free love, and no opportunity exists for propaganda against these opinions. The result is that in Russia one set of fanatics feels absolute certainty about one set of doubtful propositions, while in the rest of the world another set of fanatics feels equal certainty about a diametrically opposite set of equally doubtful propositions. From such a situation war, bitterness, and persecution inevitably result on both sides.

William James used to preach the "will to believe." For my part, I should wish to preach the "will to doubt." None of our beliefs are quite true; all have at least a penumbra of vagueness and error. The methods of increasing the degree of truth in our beliefs are well known; they consist in hearing all sides, trying to ascertain all the relevant facts, controlling our own bias by discussion with people who have the opposite bias, and cultivating a readiness to discard any hypothesis which has proved inadequate. These methods are practised in science, and have built up the body of scientific knowledge. Every man of science whose outlook is truly scientific is ready to admit that what passes for scientific knowledge at the moment is sure to require correction with the progress of discovery; nevertheless, it is near enough to the truth to serve for most practical purposes, though not for all. In science, where alone something approximating to genuine knowledge is to be found, men's attitude is tentative and full of doubt.

In religion and politics, on the contrary, though there is as yet nothing approaching scientific knowledge, everybody considers it *de rigueur* to have a dogmatic opinion, to be backed up by inflicting starvation, prison, and war, and to be carefully guarded from argumentative competition with any different opinion. If only men could be brought into a tentatively agnostic frame of mind about these matters, nine-tenths of the evils of the modern world would be cured. War would become impossible, because each side would realize that both sides must be in the wrong. Persecution would cease. Education would aim at expanding the mind, not at narrowing it. Men would be chosen for jobs on account of fitness to do the work, not because they flattered the irrational dogmas of those in power. Thus rational doubt alone, if it could be generated, would suffice to introduce the millennium.

We have had in recent years a brilliant example of the scientific temper of mind in the theory of relativity and its reception by the world. Einstein, a German-Swiss-Jew pacifist, was appointed to a research professorship by the German Government in the early days of the War; his predictions were verified by an English expedition which observed the eclipse of 1919, very soon after the Armistice. His theory upsets the whole theoretical framework of traditional physics; it is almost as damaging to orthodox dynamics as Darwin was to *Genesis*. Yet physicists everywhere have shown complete readiness to accept his theory as soon as it appeared that the evidence was in its favour.

But none of them, least of all Einstein himself, would claim that he has said the last word. He has not built a monument of infallible dogma to stand for all time. There are difficulties he cannot solve; his doctrines will have to be modified in their turn as they have modified Newton's. This critical undogmatic receptiveness is the true attitude of science.

What would have happened if Einstein had advanced something equally new in the sphere of religion or politics? English people would have found elements of Prussianism in his theory; anti-Semites would have regarded it as a Zionist plot; nationalists in all countries would have found it tainted with lily-livered pacifism, and proclaimed it a mere dodge for escaping military service. All the old-fashioned professors would have approached Scotland Yard to get the importation of his writings prohibited. Teachers favourable to him would have been dismissed. He, meantime, would have captured the Government of some backward country, where it would have become illegal to teach anything except his doctrine, which would have grown into a mysterious dogma not understood by anybody. Ultimately the truth or falsehood of his doctrine would be decided on the battlefield, without the collection of any fresh evidence for or against it. This method is the logical outcome of William James's will to believe.

What is wanted is not the will to believe, but the wish to find out, which is its exact opposite.

If it is admitted that a condition of rational doubt would be desirable, it becomes important to inquire how it comes about that there is so much irrational certainty in the world. A great deal of this is due to the inherent irrationality and credulity of average human nature. But this seed of intellectual original sin is nourished and fostered by other agencies, among which three play the chief part—namely, education, propaganda, and economic pressure. Let us consider these in turn.

(1) *Education.*—Elementary education, in all advanced countries, is in the hands of the State. Some of the things taught are known to be false by the officials who prescribe them, and many others are known to be false, or at any rate very doubtful, by every unprejudiced person. Take, for example, the teaching of history. Each nation aims only at self-glorification in the school text-books of history. When a man writes his autobiography he is expected to show a certain modesty; but when a nation writes its autobiography there is no limit to its boasting and vainglory. When I was young, school books taught that the French were wicked and the Germans virtuous; now they teach the opposite. In neither case is there the slightest regard for truth. German school books, dealing with the battle of Waterloo, represent Wellington as all but defeated when Blücher saved the situation; English books represent Blücher as having made very little difference. The writers of both the German and the English books know that they are not telling the truth. American school books used to be violently anti-British; since the War they have become equally pro-British, without aiming at truth in either case (see *The Freeman*, Feb. 15, 1922, p. 532). Both before and since, one of the chief purposes of education in the United States has been to turn the motley collection of immigrant children into "good Americans." Apparently it has not occurred to any one that a "good American," like a "good German" or a "good Japanese," must be, *pro tanto*, a bad human being. A "good American" is a man or woman imbued with the belief that America is the finest country on earth, and ought always

to be enthusiastically supported in any quarrel. It is just possible that these propositions are true; if so, a rational man will have no quarrel with them. But if they are true, they ought to be taught everywhere, not only in America. It is a suspicious circumstance that such propositions are never believed outside the particular country which they glorify. Meanwhile the whole machinery of the State, in all the different countries, is turned on to making defenceless children believe absurd propositions the effect of which is to make them willing to die in defence of sinister interests under the impression that they are fighting for truth and right. This is only one of countless ways in which education is designed, not to give true knowledge, but to make the people pliable to the will of their masters. Without an elaborate system of deceit in the elementary schools it would be impossible to preserve the camouflage of democracy.

Before leaving the subject of education, I will take another example from America[3]—not because America is any worse than other countries, but because it is the most modern, showing the dangers that are growing rather than those that are diminishing. In the State of New York a school cannot be established without a licence from the State, even if it is to be supported wholly by private funds. A recent law decrees that a licence shall not be granted to any school "where it shall appear that the instruction proposed to be given includes the teachings of the doctrine that organized Governments shall be overthrown by force, violence, or unlawful means." As the *New Republic* points out, there is no limitation to this or that organized Government. The law therefore would have made it illegal, during the War,

---

3   See *The New Republic*, Feb. 1, 1922, p. 259 *ff.*

to teach the doctrine that the Kaiser's Government should be overthrown by force; and, since then, the support of Kolchak or Denikin against the Soviet Government would have been illegal. Such consequences, of course, were not intended, and result only from bad draughtsmanship. What was intended appears from another law passed at the same time, applying to teachers in State schools. This law provides that certificates permitting persons to teach in such schools shall be issued only to those who have "shown satisfactorily" that they are "loyal and obedient to the Government of this State and of the United States," and shall be refused to those who have advocated, no matter where or when, "a form of government other than the Government of this State or of the United States." The committee which framed these laws, as quoted by the *New Republic*, laid it down that the teacher who "does not approve of the present social system......must surrender his office," and that "no person who is not eager to combat the theories of social change should be entrusted with the task of fitting the young and old for the responsibilities of citizenship." Thus, according to the law of the State of New York, Christ and George Washington were too degraded morally to be fit for the education of the young. If Christ were to go to New York and say, "Suffer the little children to come unto me," the President of the New York School Board would reply: "Sir, I see no evidence that you are eager to combat theories of social change. Indeed, I have heard it said that you advocate what you call the *kingdom* of heaven, whereas this country, thank God, is a republic. It is clear that the Government of your kingdom of heaven would differ materially from that of New York State, therefore no children will be allowed access to you." If he failed to make this reply, he would not be doing his duty as a functionary entrusted with the administration of the law.

The effect of such laws is very serious. Let it be granted, for the sake of argument, that the government and the social system in the State of New York are the best that have ever existed on this planet; yet even then both would presumably be capable of improvement. Any person who admits this obvious proposition is by law incapable of teaching in a State school. Thus the law decrees that the teachers shall all be either hypocrites or fools.

The growing danger exemplified by the New York law is that resulting from the monopoly of power in the hands of a single organization, whether the State or a Trust or federation of Trusts. In the case of education, the power is in the hands of the State, which can prevent the young from hearing of any doctrine which it dislikes. I believe there are still some people who think that a democratic State is scarcely distinguishable from the people. This, however, is a delusion. The State is a collection of officials, different for different purposes, drawing comfortable incomes so long as the *status quo* is preserved. The only alteration they are likely to desire in the *status quo* is an increase of bureaucracy and of the power of bureaucrats. It is, therefore, natural that they should take advantage of such opportunities as war excitement to acquire inquisitorial powers over their employees, involving the right to inflict starvation upon any subordinate who opposes them. In matters of the mind, such as education, this state of affairs is fatal. It puts an end to all possibility of progress or freedom or intellectual initiative. Yet it is the natural result of allowing the whole of elementary education to fall under the sway of a single organization.

Religious toleration, to a certain extent, has been won because people have ceased to consider religion so important as it was once thought to be. But in politics and economics, which have taken the place formerly occupied by religion, there is a growing tendency to persecution, which is not by any means confined to one party. The persecution of opinion in Russia is more severe than in any capitalist country. I met in Petrograd an eminent Russian poet, Alexander Block, who has since died as the result of privations. The Bolsheviks allowed him to teach æsthetics, but he complained that they insisted on his teaching the subject "from a Marxian point of view." He had been at a loss to discover how the theory of rhythmics was connected with Marxism, although, to avoid starvation, he had done his best to find out. Of course, it has been impossible in Russia ever since the Bolsheviks came into power to print anything critical of the dogmas upon which their regime is founded.

The examples of America and Russia illustrate the conclusion to which we seem to be driven—namely, that so long as men continue to have the present fanatical belief in the importance of politics free thought on political matters will be impossible, and there is only too much danger that the lack of freedom will spread to all other matters, as it has done in Russia. Only some degree of political scepticism can save us from this misfortune.

It must not be supposed that the officials in charge of education desire the young to become educated. On the contrary, their problem is to impart information without imparting intelligence. Education should have two objects: first, to give definite knowledge—reading and writing, languages and mathematics, and so on; secondly, to create those mental habits which will enable people to acquire knowledge and form sound judgments for themselves. The first of these we may call information, the second intelligence. The utility of information is admitted practically as well as theoretically; without a literate population a modern State is impossible. But the utility of intelligence is admitted only theoretically, not practically; it is not desired that ordinary people should think for themselves, because it is felt that people who think for themselves are awkward to manage and cause administrative difficulties. Only the guardians, in Plato's language, are to think; the rest are to obey, or to follow leaders like a herd of sheep. This doctrine, often unconsciously, has survived the introduction of political democracy, and has radically vitiated all national systems of education.

The country which has succeeded best in giving information without intelligence is the latest addition to modern civilization, Japan. Elementary education in Japan is said to be admirable from the point of view of instruction. But, in addition to instruction, it has another purpose, which is to teach worship of the Mikado—a far stronger creed now than before Japan became modernized.[4] Thus the schools have been used simultaneously to confer knowledge and to promote superstition. Since we are not tempted to Mikado-worship, we see clearly what is absurd in Japanese teaching. Our own national superstitions strike us as natural and sensible, so that we do not take such a true view of them as we do of the superstitions of Nippon. But if a travelled Japanese were to maintain the thesis that our schools teach

---

4   See *The Invention of a New Religion*. By Professor Chamberlain, of Tokio. Published by the Rationalist Press Association. (Now out of print.)

superstitions just as inimical to intelligence as belief in the divinity of the Mikado, I suspect that he would be able to make out a very good case.

For the present I am not in search of remedies, but am only concerned with diagnosis. We are faced with the paradoxical fact that education has become one of the chief obstacles to intelligence and freedom of thought. This is due primarily to the fact that the State claims a monopoly; but that is by no means the sole cause.

(2) *Propaganda.*—Our system of education turns young people out of the schools able to read, but for the most part unable to weigh evidence or to form an independent opinion. They are then assailed, throughout the rest of their lives, by statements designed to make them believe all sorts of absurd propositions, such as that Blank's pills cure all ills, that Spitzbergen is warm and fertile, and that Germans eat corpses. The art of propaganda, as practised by modern politicians and governments, is derived from the art of advertisement. The science of psychology owes a great deal to advertisers. In former days most psychologists would probably have thought that a man could not convince many people of the excellence of his own wares by merely stating emphatically that they were excellent. Experience shows, however, that they were mistaken in this. If I were to stand up once in a public place and state that I am the most modest man alive, I should be laughed at; but if I could raise enough money to make the same statement on all the busses and on hoardings along all the principal railway lines, people would presently become convinced that I had an abnormal shrinking from publicity. If I were to go to a small shopkeeper and say: "Look at your competitor over the way, he is getting your business; don't you think it

would be a good plan to leave your business and stand up in the middle of the road and try to shoot him before he shoots you?"—if I were to say this, any small shopkeeper would think me mad. But when the Government says it with emphasis and a brass band, the small shopkeepers become enthusiastic, and are quite surprised when they find afterwards that business has suffered. Propaganda, conducted by the means which advertisers have found successful, is now one of the recognized methods of government in all advanced countries, and is especially the method by which democratic opinion is created.

There are two quite different evils about propaganda as now practised. On the one hand, its appeal is generally to irrational causes of belief rather than to serious argument; on the other hand, it gives an unfair advantage to those who can obtain most publicity, whether through wealth or through power. For my part, I am inclined to think that too much fuss is sometimes made about the fact that propaganda appeals to emotion rather than reason. The line between emotion and reason is not so sharp as some people think. Moreover, a clever man could frame a sufficiently rational argument in favour of any position which has any chance of being adopted. There are always good arguments on both sides of any real issue. Definite mis-statements of fact can be legitimately objected to, but they are by no means necessary. The mere words "Pear's Soap," which affirm nothing, cause people to buy that article. If, wherever these words appear, they were replaced by the words "The Labour Party," millions of people would be led to vote for the Labour Party, although the advertisements had claimed no merit for it whatever. But if both sides in a controversy were confined by law to statements which a committee of eminent logicians considered relevant and valid, the main evil of propaganda, as at present conducted, would remain. Suppose, under such a law, two parties with an equally good case, one of whom had a million pounds to spend on propaganda, while the other had only a hundred thousand. It is obvious that the arguments in favour of the richer party would become more widely known than those in favour of the poorer party, and therefore the richer party would win. This situation is, of course, intensified when one party is the Government. In Russia the Government has an almost complete monopoly of propaganda, but that is not necessary. The advantages which it possesses over its opponents will generally be sufficient to give it the victory, unless it has an exceptionally bad case.

The objection to propaganda is not only its appeal to unreason, but still more the unfair advantage which it gives to the rich and powerful. Equality of opportunity among opinions is essential if there is to be real freedom of thought; and equality of opportunity among opinions can only be secured by elaborate laws directed to that end, which there is no reason to expect to see enacted. The cure is not to be sought primarily in such laws, but in better education and a more sceptical public opinion. For the moment, however, I am not concerned to discuss cures.

(3) *Economic pressure.*—I have already dealt with some aspects of this obstacle to freedom of thought, but I wish now to deal with it on more general lines, as a danger which is bound to increase unless very definite steps are taken to counteract it. The supreme example of economic pressure applied against freedom of thought is Soviet Russia, where, until the trade agreement, the Government could and did inflict starvation upon people whose opinions

it disliked—for example, Kropotkin. But in this respect Russia is only somewhat ahead of other countries. In France, during the Dreyfus affair, any teacher would have lost his position if he had been in favour of Dreyfus at the start or against him at the end. In America at the present day I doubt if a university professor, however eminent, could get employment if he were to criticize the Standard Oil Company, because all college presidents have received or hope to receive benefactions from Mr. Rockefeller. Throughout America Socialists are marked men, and find it extremely difficult to obtain work unless they have great gifts. The tendency, which exists wherever industrialism is well developed, for trusts and monopolies to control all industry, leads to a diminution of the number of possible employers, so that it becomes easier and easier to keep secret black books by means of which any one not subservient to the great corporations can be starved. The growth of monopolies is introducing in America many of the evils associated with State Socialism as it has existed in Russia. From the standpoint of liberty, it makes no difference to a man whether his only possible employer is the State or a Trust.

In America, which is the most advanced country industrially, and to a lesser extent in other countries which are approximating to the American condition, it is necessary for the average citizen, if he wishes to make a living, to avoid incurring the hostility of certain big men. And these big men have an outlook—religious, moral, and political— with which they expect their employees to agree, at least outwardly. A man who openly dissents from Christianity, or believes in a relaxation of the marriage laws, or objects to the power of the great corporations, finds America a very uncomfortable country, unless he happens to be an eminent writer. Exactly the same kind of restraints upon freedom of thought are bound to occur in every country where economic organization has been carried to the point of practical monopoly. Therefore the safeguarding of liberty in the world which is growing up is far more difficult than it was in the nineteenth century, when free competition was still a reality. Whoever cares about the freedom of the mind must face this situation fully and frankly, realizing the inapplicability of methods which answered well enough while industrialism was in its infancy.

There are two simple principles which, if they were adopted, would solve almost all social problems. The first is that education should have for one of its aims to teach people only to believe propositions when there is some reason to think that they are true. The second is that jobs should be given solely for fitness to do the work.

To take the second point first. The habit of considering a man's religious, moral, and political opinions before appointing him to a post or giving him a job is the modern form of persecution, and it is likely to become quite as efficient as the Inquisition ever was. The old liberties can be legally retained without being of the slightest use. If, in practice, certain opinions lead a man to starve, it is poor comfort to him to know that his opinions are not punishable by law. There is a certain public feeling against starving men for not belonging to the Church of England, or for holding slightly unorthodox opinions in politics. But there is hardly any feeling against the rejection of Atheists or Mormons, extreme communists, or men who advocate free love. Such men are thought to be wicked, and it is considered only natural to refuse to employ them. People have hardly yet waked up to the fact that this refusal, in a highly industrial State, amounts to a very rigorous form of persecution.

If this danger were adequately realized, it would be possible to rouse public opinion, and to secure that a man's beliefs should not be considered in appointing him to a post. The protection of minorities is vitally important; and even the most orthodox of us may find himself in a minority some day, so that we all have an interest in restraining the tyranny of majorities. Nothing except public opinion can solve this problem. Socialism would make it somewhat more acute, since it would eliminate the opportunities that now arise through exceptional employers. Every increase in the size of industrial undertakings makes it worse, since it diminishes the number of independent employers. The battle must be fought exactly as the battle of religious toleration was fought. And as in that case, so in this, a decay in the intensity of belief is likely to prove the decisive factor. While men were convinced of the absolute truth of Catholicism or Protestantism, as the case might be, they were willing to persecute on account of them. While men are quite certain of their modern creeds, they will persecute on their behalf. Some element of doubt is essential to the practice, though not to the theory, of toleration. And this brings me to my other point, which concerns the aims of education.

If there is to be toleration in the world, one of the things taught in schools must be the habit of weighing evidence, and the practice of not giving full assent to propositions which there is no reason to believe true. For example, the art of reading the newspapers should be taught. The schoolmaster should select some incident which happened a good many years ago, and roused political passions in its day. He should then read to the school children what was said by the newspapers on one side, what was said by those on the other, and some impartial account of what really happened. He should show how, from the biased account of either side, a practised reader could infer what really happened, and he should make them understand that everything in newspapers is more or less untrue. The cynical scepticism which would result from this teaching would make the children in later life immune from those appeals to idealism by which decent people are induced to further the schemes of scoundrels.

History should be taught in the same way. Napoleon's campaigns of 1813 and 1814, for instance, might be studied in the *Moniteur*, leading up to the surprise which Parisians felt when they saw the Allies arriving under the walls of Paris after they had (according to the official bulletins) been beaten by Napoleon in every battle. In the more advanced classes, students should be encouraged to count the number of times that Lenin has been assassinated by Trotsky, in order to learn contempt for death. Finally, they should be given a school history approved by the Government, and asked to infer what a French school history would say about our wars with France. All this would be a far better training in citizenship than the trite moral maxims by which some people believe that civic duty can be inculcated.

It must, I think, be admitted that the evils of the world are due to moral defects quite as much as to lack of intelligence. But the human race has not hitherto discovered any method of eradicating moral defects; preaching and exhortation only add hypocrisy to the previous list of vices. Intelligence, on the contrary, is easily improved by methods known to every competent educator. Therefore, until some method of teaching virtue has been discovered, progress will have to be sought by improvement of intelligence rather than of morals. One of the chief obstacles to intelligence is credulity, and credulity could be enormously diminished by instruction as to the prevalent forms of mendacity. Credulity is a greater evil in the present day than it ever was before, because, owing to the growth of education, it is much easier than it used to be to spread misinformation, and, owing to democracy, the spread of misinformation is more important than in former times to the holders of power. Hence the increase in the circulation of newspapers.

If I am asked how the world is to be induced to adopt these two maxims—namely (1) that jobs should be given to people on account of their fitness to perform them; (2) that one aim of education should be to cure people of the habit of believing propositions for which there is no evidence—I can only say that it must be done by generating an enlightened public opinion. And an enlightened public opinion can only be generated by the efforts of those who desire that it should exist. I do not believe that the economic changes advocated by Socialists will, of themselves, do anything towards curing the evils we have been considering. I think that, whatever happens in politics, the trend of economic development will make the preservation of mental freedom increasingly difficult, unless public opinion insists that the employer shall control nothing in the life of the employee except his work. Freedom in education could easily be secured, if it were desired, by limiting the function of the State to inspection and payment, and confining inspection rigidly to the definite instruction. But that, as things stand, would leave education in the hands of the Churches, because, unfortunately, they are more anxious to teach their beliefs than Freethinkers are to teach their doubts. It would, however, give a free field, and would make it possible for a liberal education to be given if it were really desired. More than that ought not to be asked of the law.

My plea throughout this address has been for the spread of the scientific temper, which is an altogether different thing from the knowledge of scientific results. The scientific temper is capable of regenerating mankind and providing an issue for all our troubles. The results of science, in the form of mechanism, poison gas, and the yellow press, bid fair to lead to the total downfall of our civilization. It is a curious antithesis, which a Martian might contemplate with amused detachment. But for us it is a matter of life and death. Upon its issue depends the question whether our grandchildren are to live in a happier world, or are to exterminate each other by scientific methods, leaving perhaps to negroes and Papuans the future destinies of mankind.

APPENDIX

THE CONWAY MEMORIAL LECTURESHIP

At a general meeting of the South Place Ethical Society, held on October 22, 1908, it was resolved, after full discussion, that an effort should be made to establish a series of lectures, to be printed and widely circulated, as a permanent Memorial to Dr. Conway.

Moncure Conway's untiring zeal for the emancipation of the human mind from the thraldom of obsolete or waning beliefs, his pleadings for sympathy with the oppressed and for a wider and profounder conception of human fraternity than the world has yet reached, claim, it is urged, an offering of gratitude more permanent than the eloquent obituary or reverential service of mourning.

The range of the lectures (of which the thirteenth is published herewith) must be regulated by the financial support accorded to the scheme; but it is hoped that sufficient funds will be eventually forthcoming for the endowment of periodical lectures by distinguished public men, to further the cause of social, political, and religious freedom, with which Dr. Conway's name must ever be associated.

The Conway Memorial Lecture Committee, although

not yet in possession of the necessary capital for the permanent endowment of the Lectureship, have inaugurated and maintained the work while inviting further contributions. The funds in hand, together with those which may reasonably be expected from supporters of the Movement, will ensure the delivery of an annual lecture for some years at least.

The Committee earnestly appeal for either donations or subscriptions from year to year until the Memorial is permanently established. Contributions may be forwarded to the Hon. Treasurer.

On behalf of the Executive Committee:—

(MRS.) C. FLETCHER SMITH and ERNEST CARR, *Hon. Secretaries.*

(MRS.) F. M. COCKBURN, *Hon. Treasurer,* "Peradeniya," Northampton Road, Croydon.

MYSTICISM AND LOGIC

MYSTICISM AND LOGIC

METAPHYSICS, OR THE attempt to conceive the world as a whole by means of thought, has been developed, from the first, by the union and conflict of two very different human impulses, the one urging men towards mysticism, the other urging them towards science. Some men have achieved greatness through one of these impulses alone, others through the other alone: in Hume, for example, the scientific impulse reigns quite unchecked, while in Blake a strong hostility to science co-exists with profound mystic insight. But the greatest men who have been philosophers have felt the need both of science and of mysticism: the attempt to harmonise the two was what made their life, and what always must, for all its arduous uncertainty, make philosophy, to some minds, a greater thing than either science or religion.

Before attempting an explicit characterisation of the scientific and the mystical impulses, I will illustrate them by examples from two philosophers whose greatness lies in the very intimate blending which they achieved. The two philosophers I mean are Heraclitus and Plato.

Heraclitus, as every one knows, was a believer in universal flux: time builds and destroys all things. From the few fragments that remain, it is not easy to discover how he arrived at his opinions, but there are some sayings that strongly suggest scientific observation as the source.

"The things that can be seen, heard, and learned," he says, "are what I prize the most." This is the language of the empiricist, to whom observation is the sole guarantee of truth. "The sun is new every day," is another fragment; and this opinion, in spite of its paradoxical character, is obviously inspired by scientific reflection, and no doubt seemed to him to obviate the difficulty of understanding how the sun can work its way underground from west to east during the night. Actual observation must also have suggested to him his central doctrine, that Fire is the one permanent substance, of which all visible things are passing phases. In combustion we see things change utterly, while their flame and heat rise up into the air and vanish.

"This world, which is the same for all," he says, "no one of gods or men has made; but it was ever, is now, and ever shall be, an ever-living Fire, with measures kindling, and measures going out."

"The transformations of Fire are, first of all, sea; and half of the sea is earth, half whirlwind."

This theory, though no longer one which science can accept, is nevertheless scientific in spirit. Science, too, might have inspired the famous saying to which Plato alludes: "You cannot step twice into the same rivers; for fresh waters are ever flowing in upon you." But we find also another statement among the extant fragments: "We step and do not step into the same rivers; we are and are not."

The comparison of this statement, which is mystical, with the one quoted by Plato, which is scientific, shows how intimately the two tendencies are blended in the system of Heraclitus. Mysticism is, in essence, little more than a certain intensity and depth of feeling in regard to what is believed about the universe; and this kind of feeling leads Heraclitus, on the basis of his science, to strangely poignant sayings concerning life and the world, such as:

"Time is a child playing draughts, the kingly power is a child's."

It is poetic imagination, not science, which presents Time as despotic lord of the world, with all the irresponsible frivolity of a child. It is mysticism, too, which leads Heraclitus to assert the identity of opposites: "Good and ill are one," he says; and again: "To God all things are fair and good and right, but men hold some things wrong and some right."

Much of mysticism underlies the ethics of Heraclitus. It is true that a scientific determinism alone might have inspired the statement: "Man's character is his fate"; but only a mystic would have said:

"Every beast is driven to the pasture with blows"; and again:

"It is hard to fight with one's heart's desire. What ever it wishes to get, it purchases at the cost of soul"; and again:

"Wisdom is one thing. It is to know the thought by which all things are steered through all things."[1]

Examples might be multiplied, but those that have been given are enough to show the character of the man: the facts of science, as they appeared to him, fed the flame in his soul, and in its light he saw into the depths of the world by the reflection of his own dancing swiftly penetrating fire. In such a nature we see the true union of the mystic and the

1   All the above quotations are from Burnet's *Early Greek Philosophy* (2nd ed., 1908), pp. 146–156.

man of science—the highest eminence, as I think, that it is possible to achieve in the world of thought.

In Plato, the same twofold impulse exists, though the mystic impulse is distinctly the stronger of the two, and secures ultimate victory whenever the conflict is sharp. His description of the cave is the classical statement of belief in a knowledge and reality truer and more real than that of the senses:

> Imagine[2] a number of men living in an underground cavernous chamber, with an entrance open to the light, extending along the entire length of the cavern, in which they have been confined, from their childhood, with their legs and necks so shackled that they are obliged to sit still and look straight forwards, because their chains render it impossible for them to turn their heads round: and imagine a bright fire burning some way off, above and behind them, and an elevated roadway passing between the fire and the prisoners, with a low wall built along it, like the screens which conjurors put up in front of their audience, and above which they exhibit their wonders.
>
> I have it, he replied.
>
> Also figure to yourself a number of persons walking behind this wall, and carrying with them statues of men, and images of other animals, wrought in wood and stone and all kinds of materials, together with various other articles, which overtop the wall; and, as you might expect, let some of the passers-by be talking, and others silent.

---

2   *Republic*, 514, translated by Davies and Vaughan.

You are describing a strange scene, and strange prisoners.

They resemble us, I replied.

Now consider what would happen if the course of nature brought them a release from their fetters, and a remedy for their foolishness, in the following manner. Let us suppose that one of them has been released, and compelled suddenly to stand up, and turn his neck round and walk with open eyes towards the light; and let us suppose that he goes through all these actions with pain, and that the dazzling splendour renders him incapable of discerning those objects of which he used formerly to see the shadows. What answer should you expect him to make, if some one were to tell him that in those days he was watching foolish phantoms, but that now he is somewhat nearer to reality, and is turned towards things more real, and sees more correctly; above all, if he were to point out to him the several objects that are passing by, and question him, and compel him to answer what they are? Should you not expect him to be puzzled, and to regard his old visions as truer than the objects now forced upon his notice?

Yes, much truer....

Hence, I suppose, habit will be necessary to enable him to perceive objects in that upper world. At first he will be most successful in distinguishing shadows; then he will discern the reflections of men and other things in water, and afterwards the realities; and after this he will raise his eyes to encounter the light of the moon and stars, finding it less difficult to study the heavenly bodies and the heaven itself by night, than the sun and the sun's light by day.

Doubtless.

Last of all, I imagine, he will be able to observe and contemplate the nature of the sun, not as it *appears* in water or on alien ground, but as it is in itself in its own territory.

Of course.

His next step will be to draw the conclusion, that the sun is the author of the seasons and the years, and the guardian of all things in the visible world, and in a manner the cause of all those things which he and his companions used to see.

Obviously, this will be his next step....

Now this imaginary case, my dear Glancon, you must apply in all its parts to our former statements, by comparing the region which the eye reveals, to the prison house, and the light of the fire therein to the power of the sun: and if, by the upward ascent and the contemplation of the upper world, you understand the mounting of the soul into the intellectual region, you will hit the tendency of my own surmises, since you desire to be told what they are; though, indeed, God only knows whether they are correct. But, be that as it may, the view which I take of the subject is to the following effect. In the world of knowledge, the essential Form of Good is the limit of our enquiries, and can barely be perceived; but, when perceived, we cannot help concluding that it is in every case the source of all that is bright and beautiful,—in the visible world giving birth to light and its master, and in the intellectual world dispensing, immediately and with full authority, truth and reason;—and that whosoever would act wisely, either in private or in public, must set this Form of Good before his eyes.

But in this passage, as throughout most of Plato's teaching, there is an identification of the good with the truly real, which became embodied in the philosophical tradition, and is still largely operative in our own day. In thus allowing a legislative function to the good, Plato produced a divorce between philosophy and science, from which, in my opinion, both have suffered ever since and are still suffering. The man of science, whatever his hopes may be, must lay them aside while he studies nature; and the philosopher, if he is to achieve truth must do the same. Ethical considerations can only legitimately appear when the truth has been ascertained: they can and should appear as determining our feeling towards the truth, and our manner of ordering our lives in view of the truth, but not as themselves dictating what the truth is to be.

There are passages in Plato—among those which illustrate the scientific side of his mind—where he seems clearly aware of this. The most noteworthy is the one in which Socrates, as a young man, is explaining the theory of ideas to Parmenides.

After Socrates has explained that there is an idea of the good, but not of such things as hair and mud and dirt, Parmenides advises him "not to despise even the meanest things," and this advice shows the genuine scientific temper. It is with this impartial temper that the mystic's apparent insight into a higher reality and a hidden good has to be combined if philosophy is to realise its greatest possibilities. And it is failure in this respect that has made so much of idealistic philosophy thin, lifeless, and insubstantial. It is only in marriage with the world that our ideals can bear fruit: divorced from it, they remain barren. But marriage with the world is not to be achieved by an ideal which shrinks from fact, or demands in advance that the world shall conform to its desires.

Parmenides himself is the source of a peculiarly interesting strain of mysticism which pervades Plato's thought—the mysticism which may be called "logical" because it is embodied in theories on logic. This form of mysticism, which appears, so far as the West is concerned, to have originated with Parmenides, dominates the reasonings of all the great mystical metaphysicians from his day to that of Hegel and his modern disciples. Reality, he says, is uncreated, indestructible, unchanging, indivisible; it is "immovable in the bonds of mighty chains, without beginning and without end; since coming into being and passing away have been driven afar, and true belief has cast them away." The fundamental principle of his inquiry is stated in a sentence which would not be out of place in Hegel: "Thou canst not know what is not—that is impossible—nor utter it; for it is the same thing that can be thought and that can be." And again: "It needs must be that what can be thought and spoken of is; for it is possible for it to be, and it is not possible for what is nothing to be." The impossibility of change follows from this principle; for what is past can be spoken of, and therefore, by the principle, still is.

Mystical philosophy, in all ages and in all parts of the world, is characterised by certain beliefs which are illustrated by the doctrines we have been considering.

There is, first, the belief in insight as against discursive analytic knowledge: the belief in a way of wisdom, sudden, penetrating, coercive, which is contrasted with the slow and fallible study of outward appearance by a science relying wholly upon the senses. All who are capable of absorption in an inward passion must have experienced at times the strange feeling of unreality in common objects, the loss of contact with daily things, in which the solidity of the outer world is lost, and the soul seems, in utter loneliness, to bring forth, out of its own depths, the mad dance of fantastic phantoms which have hitherto appeared as independently real and living. This is the negative side of the mystic's initiation: the doubt concerning common knowledge, preparing the way for the reception of what seems a higher wisdom. Many men to whom this negative experience is familiar do not pass beyond it, but for the mystic it is merely the gateway to an ampler world.

The mystic insight begins with the sense of a mystery unveiled, of a hidden wisdom now suddenly become certain beyond the possibility of a doubt. The sense of certainty and revelation comes earlier than any definite belief. The definite beliefs at which mystics arrive are the result of reflection upon the inarticulate experience gained in the moment of insight. Often, beliefs which have no real connection with this moment become subsequently attracted into the central nucleus; thus in addition to the convictions which all mystics share, we find, in many of them, other convictions of a more local and temporary character, which no doubt become amalgamated with what was essentially mystical in virtue of their subjective certainty. We may ignore such inessential accretions, and confine ourselves to the beliefs which all mystics share.

The first and most direct outcome of the moment of illumination is belief in the possibility of a way of knowledge which may be called revelation or insight or intuition, as contrasted with sense, reason, and analysis, which are regarded as blind guides leading to the morass of illusion. Closely connected with this belief is the conception of a Reality behind the world of appearance and utterly different from it. This Reality is regarded with an admiration often amounting to worship; it is felt to be always and everywhere close at hand, thinly veiled by the shows of sense, ready, for the receptive mind, to shine in its glory even through the apparent folly and wickedness of Man. The poet, the artist, and the lover are seekers after that glory: the haunting beauty that they pursue is the faint reflection of its sun. But the mystic lives in the full light of the vision: what others dimly seek he knows, with a knowledge beside which all other knowledge is ignorance.

The second characteristic of mysticism is its belief in unity, and its refusal to admit opposition or division anywhere. We found Heraclitus saying "good and ill are one"; and again he says, "the way up and the way down is one and the same." The same attitude appears in the simultaneous assertion of contradictory propositions, such as: "We step and do not step into the same rivers; we are and are not." The assertion of Parmenides, that reality is one and indivisible, comes from the same impulse towards unity. In Plato, this impulse is less prominent, being held in check by his theory of ideas; but it reappears, so far as his logic permits, in the doctrine of the primacy of the Good.

A third mark of almost all mystical metaphysics is the denial of the reality of Time. This is an outcome of the denial of division; if all is one, the distinction of past and future must be illusory. We have seen this doctrine prominent in Parmenides; and among moderns it is fundamental in the systems of Spinoza and Hegel.

The last of the doctrines of mysticism which we have to consider is its belief that all evil is mere appearance, an illusion produced by the divisions and oppositions of the analytic intellect. Mysticism does not maintain that such things as cruelty, for example, are good, but it denies that they are real: they belong to that lower world of phantoms from which we are to be liberated by the insight of the vision. Sometimes—for example in Hegel, and at least verbally in Spinoza—not only evil, but good also, is regarded as illusory, though nevertheless the emotional attitude towards what is held to be Reality is such as would naturally be associated with the belief that Reality is good. What is, in all cases, ethically characteristic of mysticism is absence of indignation or protest, acceptance with joy, disbelief in the ultimate truth of the division into two hostile camps, the good and the bad. This attitude is a direct outcome of the nature of the mystical experience: with its sense of unity is associated a feeling of infinite peace. Indeed it may be suspected that the feeling of peace produces, as feelings do in dreams, the whole system of associated beliefs which make up the body of mystic doctrine. But this is a difficult question, and one on which it cannot be hoped that mankind will reach agreement.

Four questions thus arise in considering the truth or falsehood of mysticism, namely:

I. Are there two ways of knowing, which may be called respectively reason and intuition? And if so, is either to be preferred to the other?

II. Is all plurality and division illusory?

III. Is time unreal?

IV. What kind of reality belongs to good and evil?

On all four of these questions, while fully developed mysticism seems to me mistaken, I yet believe that, by sufficient restraint, there is an element of wisdom to be learned from the mystical way of feeling, which does not seem to be attainable in any other manner. If this is the truth, mysticism is to be commended as an attitude towards life, not as a creed about the world. The metaphysical creed, I shall maintain, is a mistaken outcome of the emotion, although this emotion, as colouring and informing all other thoughts and feelings, is the inspirer of whatever is best in Man. Even the cautious and patient investigation of truth by science, which seems the very antithesis of the mystic's swift certainty, may be fostered and nourished by that very spirit of reverence in which mysticism lives and moves.

I. REASON AND INTUITION[3]

OF THE REALITY or unreality of the mystic's world I know nothing. I have no wish to deny it, nor even to declare that the insight which reveals it is not a genuine insight. What I do wish to maintain—and it is here that the scientific attitude becomes imperative—is that insight, untested and unsupported, is an insufficient guarantee of truth, in spite of the fact that much of the most important truth is first suggested by its means. It is common to speak of an opposition between instinct and reason; in the eighteenth century, the opposition was drawn in favour of reason, but under the

---

3   This section, and also one or two pages in later sections, have been printed in a course of Lowell lectures *On our knowledge of the external world,* published by the Open Court Publishing Company. But I have left them here, as this is the context for which they were originally written.

influence of Rousseau and the romantic movement instinct was given the preference, first by those who rebelled against artificial forms of government and thought, and then, as the purely rationalistic defence of traditional theology became increasingly difficult, by all who felt in science a menace to creeds which they associated with a spiritual outlook on life and the world. Bergson, under the name of "intuition," has raised instinct to the position of sole arbiter of metaphysical truth. But in fact the opposition of instinct and reason is mainly illusory. Instinct, intuition, or insight is what first leads to the beliefs which subsequent reason confirms or confutes; but the confirmation, where it is possible, consists, in the last analysis, of agreement with other beliefs no less instinctive. Reason is a harmonising, controlling force rather than a creative one. Even in the most purely logical realm, it is insight that first arrives at what is new.

Where instinct and reason do sometimes conflict is in regard to single beliefs, held instinctively, and held with such determination that no degree of inconsistency with other beliefs leads to their abandonment. Instinct, like all human faculties, is liable to error. Those in whom reason is weak are often unwilling to admit this as regards themselves, though all admit it in regard to others. Where instinct is least liable to error is in practical matters as to which right judgment is a help to survival: friendship and hostility in others, for instance, are often felt with extraordinary discrimination through very careful disguises. But even in such matters a wrong impression may be given by reserve or flattery; and in matters less directly practical, such as philosophy deals with, very strong instinctive beliefs are sometimes wholly mistaken, as we may come to know through their perceived inconsistency with other equally strong beliefs.

It is such considerations that necessitate the harmonising mediation of reason, which tests our beliefs by their mutual compatibility, and examines, in doubtful cases, the possible sources of error on the one side and on the other. In this there is no opposition to instinct as a whole, but only to blind reliance upon some one interesting aspect of instinct to the exclusion of other more commonplace but not less trustworthy aspects. It is such one-sidedness, not instinct itself, that reason aims at correcting.

These more or less trite maxims may be illustrated by application to Bergson's advocacy of "intuition" as against "intellect." There are, he says, "two profoundly different ways of knowing a thing. The first implies that we move round the object: the second that we enter into it. The first depends on the point of view at which we are placed and on the symbols by which we express ourselves. The second neither depends on a point of view nor relies on any symbol. The first kind of knowledge may be said to stop at the *relative*; the second, in those cases where it is possible, to attain the *absolute*."[4] The second of these, which is intuition, is, he says, "the kind of *intellectual sympathy* by which one places oneself within an object in order to coincide with what is unique in it and therefore inexpressible" (p. 6). In illustration, he mentions self-knowledge: "there is one reality, at least, which we all seize from within, by intuition and not by simple analysis. It is our own personality in its flowing through time—our self which endures" (p. 8). The rest of Bergson's philosophy consists in reporting, through the imperfect medium of words, the knowledge gained by intuition, and the consequent complete condemnation

---

4   *Introduction to Metaphysics*, p. a.

of all the pretended knowledge derived from science and common sense.

This procedure, since it takes sides in a conflict of instinctive beliefs, stands in need of justification by proving the greater trustworthiness of the beliefs on one side than of those on the other. Bergson attempts this justification in two ways, first by explaining that intellect is a purely practical faculty to secure biological success, secondly by mentioning remarkable feats of instinct in animals and by pointing out characteristics of the world which, though intuition can apprehend them, are baffling to intellect as he interprets it.

Of Bergson's theory that intellect is a purely practical faculty, developed in the struggle for survival, and not a source of true beliefs, we may say, first, that it is only through intellect that we know of the struggle for survival and of the biological ancestry of man: if the intellect is misleading, the whole of this merely inferred history is presumably untrue. If, on the other hand, we agree with him in thinking that evolution took place as Darwin believed, then it is not only intellect, but all our faculties, that have been developed under the stress of practical utility. Intuition is seen at its best where it is directly useful, for example in regard to other people's characters and dispositions. Bergson apparently holds that capacity, for this kind of knowledge is less explicable by the struggle for existence than, for example, capacity for pure mathematics Yet the savage deceived by false friendship is likely to pay for his mistake with his life; whereas even in the most civilised societies men are not put to death for mathematical incompetence. All the most striking of his instances of intuition in animals have a very direct survival value. The fact is, of course, that both intuition and intellect have been developed because they are useful, and that, speaking broadly, they are useful when they give truth and become harmful when they give falsehood. Intellect, in civilised man, like artistic capacity, has occasionally been developed beyond the point where it is useful to the individual; intuition, on the other hand, seems on the whole to diminish as civilisation increases. It is greater, as a rule, in children than in adults, in the uneducated than in the educated. Probably in dogs it exceeds anything to be found in human beings. But those who see in these facts a recommendation of intuition ought to return to running wild in the woods, dyeing themselves with woad and living on hips and haws.

Let us next examine whether intuition possesses any such infallibility as Bergson claims for it. The best instance of it, according to him, is our acquaintance with ourselves; yet self-knowledge is proverbially rare and difficult. Most men, for example, have in their nature meannesses, vanities, and envies of which they are quite unconscious, though even their best friends can perceive them without any difficulty. It is true that intuition has a convincingness which is lacking to intellect: while it is present, it is almost impossible to doubt its truth. But if it should appear, on examination, to be at least as fallible as intellect, its greater subjective certainty becomes a demerit, making it only the more irresistibly deceptive. Apart from self-knowledge, one of the most notable examples of intuition is the knowledge people believe themselves to possess of those with whom they are in love: the wall between different personalities seems to become transparent, and people think they see into another soul as into their own. Yet deception in such cases is constantly practised with success; and even where there is no intentional deception, experience gradually proves, as a rule, that the supposed insight was illusory, and that the slower more groping methods of the intellect are in the long run more reliable.

Bergson maintains that intellect can only deal with things in so far as they resemble what has been experienced in the past, while intuition has the power of apprehending the uniqueness and novelty that always belong to each fresh moment. That there is something unique and new at every moment, is certainly true; it is also true that this cannot be fully expressed by means of intellectual concepts. Only direct acquaintance can give knowledge of what is unique and new. But direct acquaintance of this kind is given fully in sensation, and does not require, so far as I can see, any special faculty of intuition for its apprehension. It is neither intellect nor intuition, but sensation, that supplies new data; but when the data are new in any remarkable manner, intellect is much more capable of dealing with them than intuition would be. The hen with a brood of ducklings no doubt has intuition which seems to place her inside them, and not merely to know them analytically; but when the ducklings take to the water, the whole apparent intuition is seen to be illusory, and the hen is left helpless on the shore. Intuition, in fact, is an aspect and development of instinct, and, like all instinct, is admirable in those customary surroundings which have moulded the habits of the animal in question, but totally incompetent as soon as the surroundings are changed in a way which demands some non-habitual mode of action.

The theoretical understanding of the world, which is the aim of philosophy, is not a matter of great practical importance to animals, or to savages, or even to most civilised men. It is hardly to be supposed, therefore, that the rapid, rough and ready methods of instinct or intuition will find in this field a favourable ground for their application. It is the older kinds of activity, which bring out our kinship with remote generations of animal and semi-human ancestors, that show intuition at its best. In such matters as self-preservation and love, intuition will act sometimes (though not always) with a swiftness and precision which are astonishing to the critical intellect. But philosophy is not one of the pursuits which illustrate our affinity with the past: it is a highly refined, highly civilised pursuit, demanding, for its success, a certain liberation from the life of instinct, and even, at times, a certain aloofness from all mundane hopes and fears. It is not in philosophy, therefore, that we can hope to see intuition at its best. On the contrary, since the true objects of philosophy, and the habit of thought demanded for their apprehension, are strange, unusual, and remote, it is here, more almost than anywhere else, that intellect proves superior to intuition, and that quick unanalysed convictions are least deserving of uncritical acceptance.

In advocating the scientific restraint and balance, as against the self-assertion of a confident reliance upon intuition, we are only urging, in the sphere of knowledge, that largeness of contemplation, that impersonal disinterestedness, and that freedom from practical preoccupations which have been inculcated by all the great religions of the world. Thus our conclusion, however it may conflict with the explicit beliefs of many mystics, is, in essence, not contrary to the spirit which inspires those beliefs, but rather the outcome of this very spirit as applied in the realm of thought.

II. UNITY AND PLURALITY

ONE OF THE most convincing aspects of the mystic illumination is the apparent revelation of the oneness of all things, giving rise to pantheism in religion and to monism in philosophy An elaborate logic, beginning with Parmenides, and culminating in Hegel and his followers, has been gradually developed, to prove that the universe is one indivisible whole, and that what seem to be its parts, if considered as substantial and self-existing, are mere illusion. The conception of a Reality quite other than the world of appearance, a reality one, indivisible, and unchanging, was introduced into Western philosophy by Parmenides, not, nominally at least, for mystical or religious reasons, but on the basis of a logical argument as to the impossibility of not-being, and most subsequent metaphysical systems are the outcome of this fundamental idea.

The logic used in defence of mysticism seems to be faulty as logic, and open to technical criticisms, which I have explained elsewhere. I shall not here repeat these criticisms, since they are lengthy and difficult, but shall instead attempt an analysis of the state of mind from which mystical logic has arisen.

Belief in a reality quite different from what appears to the senses arises with irresistible force in certain moods, which are the source of most mysticism, and of most metaphysics While such a mood is dominant, the need of logic is not felt, and accordingly the more thorough going mystics do not employ logic, but appeal directly to the immediate deliverance of their insight. But such fully developed mysticism is rare in the West. When the intensity of emotional conviction subsides, a man who is in the habit of reasoning will search for logical grounds in favour of the belief which he finds in himself. But since the belief already exists, he will be very hospitable to any ground that suggests itself. The paradoxes apparently proved by his logic are really the paradoxes of mysticism, and are the goal which he feels his logic must reach if it is to be in accordance with insight. The resulting logic has rendered most philosophers incapable of giving any account of the world of science and daily life, If they had been anxious to give such an account, they would probably have discovered the errors of their logic; but most of them were less anxious to understand the world of science and daily life than to convict it of unreality in the interests of a super-sensible "real" world.

It is in this way that logic has been pursued by those of the great philosophers who were mystics. But since they usually took for granted the supposed insight of the mystic emotion, their logical doctrines were presented with a certain dryness, and were believed by their disciples to be quite independent of the sudden illumination from which they sprang. Nevertheless their origin clung to them, and they remained—to borrow a useful word from Mr. Santayana—"malicious" in regard to the world of science and common sense. It is only so that we can account for the complacency with which philosophers have accepted the inconsistency of their doctrines with all the common and scientific facts which seem best established and most worthy of belief.

The logic of mysticism shows, as is natural, the defects which are inherent in anything malicious. The impulse to logic, not felt while the mystic mood is dominant, reasserts itself as the mood fades, but with a desire to retain the vanishing insight, or at least to prove that it *was* insight, and that what seems to contradict it is illusion. The logic which thus arises is not quite disinterested or candid, and is inspired by a certain hatred of the daily world to which it is to be applied. Such an attitude naturally does not tend to the best results. Everyone knows that to read an author simply in order to refute him is not the way to understand him; and to read the book of Nature with a conviction that it is all illusion is just as unlikely to lead to understanding. If our logic is to find the common world intelligible, it must not be hostile, but must be inspired by a genuine acceptance such as is not usually to be found among metaphysicians.

III. TIME

THE UNREALITY OF time is a cardinal doctrine of many metaphysical systems, often nominally based, as already by Parmenides, upon logical arguments, but originally derived, at any rate in the founders of new systems, from the certainty which is born in the moment of mystic insight. As a Persian Sufi poet says:

> Past and future are what veil God from our sight.
> Burn up both of them with fire! How long
> Wilt thou be partitioned by these segments as a reed?[5]

The belief that what is ultimately real must be immutable is a very common one: it gave rise to the metaphysical notion of substance, and finds, even now, a wholly illegitimate

---

5   Whinfield's translation of the *Masnavi* (Trübner, 1887), p. 34.

satisfaction in such scientific doctrines as the conservation of energy and mass.

It is difficult to disentangle the truth and the error in this view. The arguments for the contention that time is unreal and that the world of sense is illusory must, I think, be regarded as fallacious. Nevertheless there is some sense—easier to feel than to state—in which time is an unimportant and superficial characteristic of reality. Past and future must be acknowledged to be as real as the present, and a certain emancipation from slavery to time is essential to philosophic thought. The importance of time is rather practical than theoretical, rather in relation to our desires than in relation to truth. A truer image of the world, I think, is obtained by picturing things as entering into the stream of time from an eternal world outside, than from a view which regards time as the devouring tyrant of all that is Both in thought and in feeling, even though time be real, to realise the unimportance of time is the gate of wisdom.

That this is the case may be seen at once by asking ourselves why our feelings towards the past are so different from our feelings towards the future. The reason for this difference is wholly practical: our wishes can affect the future but not the past, the future is to some extent subject to our power, while the past is unalterably fixed. But every future will some day be past: if we see the past truly now, it must, when it was still future, have been just what we now see it to be, and what is now future must be just what we shall see it to be when it has become past. The felt difference of quality between past and future, therefore, is not an intrinsic difference, but only a difference in relation to us: to impartial contemplation, it ceases to exist. And impartiality of contemplation is, in the intellectual sphere, that very same virtue of disinterestedness which, in the sphere of action, appears as justice and unselfishness. Whoever wishes to see the world truly, to rise in thought above the tyranny of practical desires, must learn to overcome the difference of attitude towards past and future, and to survey the whole stream of time in one comprehensive vision.

The kind of way in which, as it seems to me, time ought not to enter into our theoretic philosophical thought, may be illustrated by the philosophy which has become associated with the idea of evolution, and which is exemplified by Nietzsche, pragmatism, and Bergson. This philosophy, on the basis of the development which has led from the lowest forms of life up to man, sees in *progress* the fundamental law of the universe, and thus admits the difference between *earlier* and *later* into the very citadel of its contemplative outlook. With its past and future history of the world, conjectural as it is, I do not wish to quarrel. But I think that, in the intoxication of a quick success, much that is required for a true understanding of the universe has been forgotten. Something of Hellenism, something, too, of Oriental resignation, must be combined with its hurrying Western self-assertion before it can emerge from the ardour of youth into the mature wisdom of manhood. In spite of its appeals to science, the true scientific philosophy, I think, is something more arduous and more aloof, appealing to less mundane hopes, and requiring a severer discipline for its successful practice.

Darwin's *Origin of Species* persuaded the world that the difference between different species of animals and plants is not the fixed immutable difference that it appears to be. The doctrine of natural kinds, which had rendered classification easy and definite, which was enshrined in the Aristotelian tradition, and protected by its supposed necessity for orthodox dogma, was suddenly swept away for ever out of the biological world. The difference between man and the lower animals, which to our human conceit appears enormous, was shown to be a gradual achievement, involving intermediate being who could not with certainty be placed either within or with out the human family. The sun and the planets had already been shown by Laplace to be very probably derived from a primitive more or less undifferentiated nebula. Thus the old fixed landmarks became wavering and indistinct, and all sharp outlines were blurred. Things and species lost their boundaries, and none could say where they began or where they ended.

But if human conceit was staggered for a moment by its kinship with the ape, it soon found a way to reassert itself, and that way is the "philosophy" of evolution, a process which led from the amœba to Man appeared to the philosophers to be obviously a progress—though whether the amœba would agree with this opinion is not known. Hence the cycle of changes which science had shown to be the probable history of the past was welcomed as revealing a law of development towards good in the universe—an evolution or unfolding of an idea slowly embodying itself in the actual. But such a view, though it might satisfy Spencer and those whom we may call Hegelian evolutionists, could not be accepted as adequate by the more whole-hearted votaries of change. An ideal to which the world continuously approaches is, to these minds, too dead and static to be inspiring. Not only the aspiration, but the ideal too, must change and develop with the course of evolution: there must be no fixed goal, but a continual fashioning of fresh needs by the impulse which is life and which alone gives unity to the process.

Life, in this philosophy, is a continuous stream, in which all divisions are artificial and unreal. Separate things, beginnings and endings, are mere convenient fictions: there is only smooth unbroken transition. The beliefs of to-day may count as true to-day, if they carry us along the stream; but to-morrow they will be false, and must be replaced by new beliefs to meet the new situation. All our thinking consists of convenient fictions, imaginary congealings of the stream: reality flows on in spite of all our fictions, and though it can be lived, it cannot be conceived in thought. Somehow, without explicit statement, the assurance is slipped in that the future, though we cannot foresee it, will be better than the past or the present: the reader is like the child which expects a sweet because it has been told to open its mouth and shut its eyes. Logic, mathematics, physics disappear in this philosophy, because they are too "static"; what is real is no impulse and movement towards a goal which, like the rainbow, recedes as we advance, and makes every place different when it reaches it from what it appeared to be at a distance.

I do not propose to enter upon a technical examination of this philosophy. I wish only to maintain that the motives and interests which inspire it are so exclusively practical, and the problems with which it deals are so special, that it can hardly be regarded as touching any of the questions that, to my mind, constitute genuine philosophy.

The predominant interest of evolutionism is in the question of human destiny, or at least of the destiny of Life. It is more interested in morality and happiness than in knowledge for its own sake. It must be admitted that the same may be said of many other philosophies, and that a desire for the kind of knowledge which philosophy can give is very rare. But if philosophy is to attain truth, it is necessary first and foremost that philosophers should acquire the disinterested intellectual curiosity which characterises the genuine man of science. Knowledge concerning the future—which is the kind of knowledge that must be sought if we are to know about human destiny—is possible within certain narrow limits. It is impossible to say how much the limits may be enlarged with the progress of science. But what is evident is that any proposition about the future belongs by its subject-matter to some particular science, and is to be ascertained, if at all, by the methods of that science. Philosophy is not a shortcut to the same kind of results as those of the other sciences: if it is to be a genuine study, it must have a province of its own, and aim at results which the other sciences can neither prove nor disprove.

Evolutionism, in basing itself upon the notion of *progress*, which is change from the worse to the better, allows the notion of time, as it seems to me, to become its tyrant rather than its servant, and thereby loses that impartiality of contemplation which is the source of all that is best in philosophic thought and feeling. Metaphysicians, as we saw, have frequently denied altogether the reality of time. I do not wish to do this; I wish only to preserve the mental outlook which inspired the denial, the attitude which, in thought, regards the past as having the same reality as the present and the same importance as the future. "In so far," says Spinoza,[6] "as the mind conceives a thing according to the dictate of reason, it will be equally affected whether

6   *Ethics*. Bk. IV, Prop. LXII.

the idea is that of a future, past, or present thing." It is this "conceiving according to the dictate of reason" that I find lacking in the philosophy which is based on evolution.

IV. GOOD AND EVIL

MYSTICISM MAINTAINS THAT all evil is illusory, and sometimes maintains the same view as regards good, but more often holds that all Reality is good. Both views are to be found in Heraclitus: "Good and ill are one," he says, but again, "To God all things are fair and good and right, but men hold some things wrong and some right." A similar twofold position is to be found in Spinoza, but he uses the word "perfection" when he means to speak of the good that is not merely human. "By reality and perfection I mean the same thing," he says;[7] but elsewhere we find the definition: "By good I shall mean that which we certainly know to be useful to us."[8] Thus perfection belongs to Reality in its own nature, but goodness is relative to ourselves and our needs, and disappears in an impartial survey. Some such distinction, I think, is necessary in order to understand the ethical outlook of mysticism: there is a lower mundane kind of good and evil, which divides the world of appearance into what seem to be conflicting parts; but there is also a higher, mystical kind of good, which belongs to Reality and is not opposed by any correlative kind of evil.

It is difficult to give a logically tenable account of this position without recognising that good and evil are subjective,

---

7   *Ethics.* Pt. II. Df. VI.
8   Ib., Pt. IV, Df. I.

that what is good is merely that towards which we have one kind of feeling, and what is evil is merely that towards which we have another kind of feeling. In our active life, where we have to exercise choice, and to prefer this to that of two possible acts, it is necessary to have a distinction of good and evil, or at least of better and worse. But this distinction, like everything pertaining to action, belongs to what mysticism regards as the world of illusion, if only because it is essentially concerned with time. In our contemplative life, where action is not called for, it is possible to be impartial, and to overcome the ethical dualism which action requires. So long as we remain *merely* impartial, we may be content to say that both the good and the evil of action are illusions. But if, as we must do if we have the mystic vision, we find the whole world worthy of love and worship, if we see

> "The earth, and every common sight....
> Apparell'd in celestial light,"

we shall say that there is a higher good than that of action, and that this higher good belongs to the whole world as it is in reality. In this way the twofold attitude and the apparent vacillation of mysticism are explained and justified.

The possibility of this universal love and joy in all that exists is of supreme importance for the conduct and happiness of life, and gives inestimable value to the mystic emotion, apart from any creeds which may be built upon it. But if we are not to be led into false beliefs, it is necessary to realise exactly *what* the mystic emotion reveals. It reveals a possibility of human nature—a possibility of a nobler, happier, freer life than any that can be otherwise achieved. But it does not reveal anything about the non-human, or about the nature of the universe in general. Good and bad, and even the higher good that mysticism finds everywhere, are the reflections of our own emotions on other things, not part of the substance of things as they are in themselves. And therefore an impartial contemplation, freed from all pre-occupation with Self, will not judge things good or bad, although it is very easily combined with that feeling of universal love which leads the mystic to say that the whole world is good.

The philosophy of evolution, through the notion of progress, is bound up with the ethical dualism of the worse and the better, and is thus shut out, not only from the kind of survey which discards good and evil altogether from its view, but also from the mystical belief in the goodness of everything. In this way the distinction of good and evil, like time, becomes a tyrant in this philosophy, and introduces into thought the restless selectiveness of action. Good and evil, like time, are, it would seem, not general or fundamental in the world of thought, but late and highly specialised members of the intellectual hierarchy.

Although, as we saw, mysticism can be interpreted so as to agree with the view that good and evil are not intellectually fundamental, it must be admitted that here we are no longer in verbal agreement with most of the great philosophers and religious teachers of the past. I believe, however, that the elimination of ethical considerations from philosophy is both scientifically necessary and—though this may seem a paradox—an ethical advance. Both these contentions must be briefly defended.

The hope of satisfaction to our more human desires— the hope of demonstrating that the world has this or that desirable ethical characteristic—is not one which, so far as

I can see, a scientific philosophy can do anything whatever to satisfy. The difference between a good world and a bad one is a difference in the particular characteristics of the particular things that exist in these worlds: it is not a sufficiently abstract difference to come within the province of philosophy. Love and hate, for example, are ethical opposites, but to philosophy they are closely analogous attitudes towards objects. The general form and structure of those attitudes towards objects which constitute mental phenomena is a problem for philosophy, but the difference between love and hate is not a difference of form or structure, and therefore belongs rather to the special science of psychology than to philosophy. Thus the ethical interests which have often inspired philosophers must remain in the background: some kind of ethical interest may inspire the whole study, but none must obtrude in the detail or be expected in the special results which are sought.

If this view seems at first sight disappointing, we may remind ourselves that a similar change has been found necessary in all the other sciences. The physicist or chemist is not now required to prove the ethical importance of his ions or atoms; the biologist is not expected to prove the utility of the plants or animals which he dissects. In pre-scientific ages this was not the case. Astronomy, for example, was studied because men believed in astrology: it was thought that the movements of the planets had the most direct and important bearing upon the lives of human beings. Presumably, when this belief decayed and the disinterested study of astronomy began, many who had found astrology absorbingly interesting decided that astronomy had too little human interest to be worthy of study. Physics, as it appears in Plato's *Timæus* for example, is full of ethical notions: it is an essential part of its purpose to show that the earth is worthy of admiration. The modern physicist, on the contrary, though he has no wish to deny that the earth is admirable, is not concerned, as physicist, with its ethical attributes: he is merely concerned to find out facts, not to consider whether they are good or bad. In psychology, the scientific attitude is even more recent and more difficult than in the physical sciences: it is natural to consider that human nature is either good or bad, and to suppose that the difference between good and bad, so all-important in practice, must be important in theory also. It is only during the last century that an ethically neutral psychology has grown up; and here too, ethical neutrality has been essential to scientific success.

In philosophy, hitherto, ethical neutrality has been seldom sought and hardly ever achieved. Men have remembered their wishes, and have judged philosophies in relation to their wishes. Driven from the particular sciences, the belief that the notions of good and evil must afford a key to the understanding of the world has sought a refuge in philosophy. But even from this last refuge, if philosophy is not to remain a set of pleasing dreams, this belief must be driven forth. It is a commonplace that happiness is not best achieved by those who seek it directly; and it would seem that the same is true of the good. In thought, at any rate, those who forget good and evil and seek only to know the facts are more likely to achieve good than those who view the world through the distorting medium of their own desires.

We are thus brought back to our seeming paradox, that a philosophy which does not seek to impose upon the world its own conceptions of good and evil is not only more likely to achieve truth, but is also the outcome of a higher ethical standpoint than one which, like evolutionism and most traditional systems, is perpetually appraising the universe and seeking to find in it an embodiment of present ideals. In religion, and in every deeply serious view of the world and of human destiny, there is an element of submission, a realisation of the limits of human power, which is somewhat lacking in the modern world, with its quick material successes and its insolent belief in the boundless possibilities of progress. "He that loveth his life shall lose it"; and there is danger lest, through a too confident love of life, life itself should lose much of what gives it its highest worth. The submission which religion inculcates in action is essentially the same in spirit as that which science teaches in thought; and the ethical neutrality by which its victories have been achieved is the outcome of that submission.

The good which it concerns us to remember is the good which it lies in our power to create—the good in our own lives and in our attitude towards the world. Insistence on belief in an external realisation of the good is a form of self-assertion, which, while it cannot secure the external good which it desires, can seriously impair the inward good which lies within our power, and destroy that reverence towards fact which constitutes both what is valuable in humility and what is fruitful in the scientific temper.

Human beings cannot, of course, wholly transcend human nature; something subjective, if only the interest that determines the direction of our attention, must remain in all our thought. But scientific philosophy comes nearer to objectivity than any other human pursuit, and gives us, therefore, the closest constant and the most intimate relation with the outer world that it is possible to achieve. To the primitive mind, everything is either friendly or hostile; but experience has shown that friendliness and hostility are not the conceptions by which the world is to be understood. Scientific philosophy thus represents, though as yet only in a nascent condition, a higher form of thought than any pre-scientific belief or imagination, and, like every approach to self-transcendence, it brings with it a rich reward in increase of scope and breadth and comprehension. Evolutionism, in spite of its appeals to particular scientific facts, fails to be a truly scientific philosophy because of its slavery to time, its ethical preoccupations, and its predominant interest in our mundane concerns and destiny. A truly scientific philosophy will be more humble, more piece meal, more arduous, offering less glitter of outward mirage to flatter fallacious hopes, but more indifferent to fate, and more capable of accepting the world without the tyrannous imposition of our human and temporary demands.

BIOGRAPHICAL TIMELINE

1872   Bertrand Arthur William Russell (3rd Earl Russell)
        is born on May 18 in Trellech, Monmouthshire,
        Wales, into an influential aristocratic family. He is
        the son of Viscount and Viscountess Amberley, who
        are radical for their time. His father, Lord Amberley,
        is known for his unorthodox views on religion and
        for his active support of birth control and wom-
        en's suffrage, which contributed to the end of his
        short career as Liberal Member of Parliament. His
        mother, Lady Amberley, is a British suffragist and
        an early advocate of birth control in the United
        Kingdom. With her husband's consent, she has an
        affair with her children's tutor, the biologist Douglas
        Spalding. Russell is the godson of John Stuart Mill
        and the grandson of Lord John Russell (1st Earl),
        prime minister to Queen Victoria in the 1840s and
        1860s. He has two siblings: a brother, Frank, who is
        seven years older and a sister, Rachel, who is four
        years older.

1874   Mother dies of diphtheria; sister Rachel's dies shortly
        thereafter.

1876   Father dies of bronchitis after a long depression.
        Russell, age four, and his older brother Frank move
        in with their rigidly Victorian grandparents (former

Prime Minister Earl Russell and Countess Russell) in Richmond Park, London.

1883   Develops a passionate interest in mathematics after being introduced to Euclid by his brother Frank, an event that he describes in his autobiography as "one of the great events of my life, as dazzling as first love."

1887   Grandfather Lord John Russell dies, leaving the children entirely in the care of their grandmother, Countess Russell, a devout Scottish Presbyterian who successfully petitions the court to set aside a provision in Amberley's will requiring the children to be raised as agnostics. At this time, begins to doubt the validity of Christian religious dogma.

1889   Meets future wife Alys Pearsall Smith, an American Quaker five years his elder and a graduate of Bryn Mawr College near Philadelphia.

1890   Becomes an atheist after reading Mill's *Autobiography*.

Travels to European continent and visits the Eiffel Tower.

Wins a scholarship to study mathematics at Trinity College, Cambridge. While at Cambridge, meets future co-author of *Principia Mathematica*, Alfred North Whitehead, and George Edward Moore, who would become a long-time collaborator.

1893   Graduates with a first-class B.A. in mathematics.

1894   Completes the Moral Sciences Tripos at Cambridge.

Marries Alys Pearsall Smith on December 13.

1896   Publishes first work, *German Social Democracy*.

Teaches German social democracy at the London School of Economics.

1895   Studies at the University of Berlin.

1896   Appointed lecturer at the London School of Economics; lectures in the US at Johns Hopkins and Bryn Mawr.

1897   *An Essay on the Foundations of Geometry.*

1899   Appointed lecturer at Trinity College, Cambridge.

1900   *A Critical Exposition of the Philosophy of Leibniz.*

Attends the First International Congress of Philosophy in Paris and meets Giuseppe Peano whose *Formulario mathematico* is instrumental in his formulation of Russell's paradox, which he publishes the following year.

1901   Marriage to Alys Pearsall Smith begins to fall apart.

1903   Advances the famous paradox bearing his name in his work *The Principles of Mathematics;* publishes *A Free Man's Worship, and Other Essays.*

1905   Introduces the theory of descriptions in "On Denoting," which is published in the philosophical journal *Mind.*

1907   Advocates, as a candidate for Parliament, for women's suffrage. Does not win election.

1908   Elected a Fellow of the Royal Society.

1910   *Philosophical Essays;* also publishes, with Alfred North Whitehead, the three-volume *Principia Mathematica* (1910–13).

Reappointed lecturer at Trinity College, Cambridge; is passed over for a Fellowship because of his "anti-clerical" views. Teaches and mentors Ludwig Wittgenstein.

1911 Separates from Alys Pearsall Smith; begins affair with Lady Ottoline Morrell, a society hostess and patron of writers such as Aldous Huxley, Siegfried Sassoon, T. S. Eliot, and D. H. Lawrence, and artists including Mark Gertler, Dora Carrington, and Gilbert Spencer. Also has simultaneous affairs with a number of other women, including, according to some, Vivienne Haigh-Wood, the English governess and writer, and first wife of T. S. Eliot.

1912 *The Problems of Philosophy.*

1913 Lectures at the École des Hautes Sociales in Paris.

1914 *Our Knowledge of the External World as a Field for Scientific Method in Philosophy.*

   Visits Harvard and teaches courses in logic and the theory of knowledge; meets T. S. Eliot.

1916 *Principles of Social Reconstruction; Why Men Fight; Justice in War-time.*

   Dismissed from Trinity College for passivist stance and agitating against British involvement in World War I, for which he is convicted under the Defence of the Realm Act 1914.

1917 *Political Ideals.*

   Plays a significant part in the Leeds Convention in June, a gathering of well over a thousand "anti-war socialists." Including delegates from the Independent Labour Party and the Socialist Party, united in their pacifist beliefs and advocating a peace settlement.

1918 "The Philosophy of Logical Atomism" (a series of eight lectures); *Mysticism and Logic and Other Essays; Proposed Roads to Freedom: Socialism, Anarchism, and Syndicalism.*

Convicted and imprisoned for five months for lecturing against inviting the United States to enter the war on the United Kingdom's side.

1919   *Introduction to Mathematical Philosophy.*

1920   In January, Russell accepts offer of reinstatement at Trinity College due to pressure by majority of the Fellows of the College. However, requests a yearlong leave of absence. Over the summer, visits Soviet Russia as part of an official delegation sent by the British government to investigate the effects of the Russian Revolution. Meets Vladimir Lenin and, in his autobiography, writes that he found Lenin disappointing, sensing an "impish cruelty" in him. His first-hand experiences destroy his previous tentative support for the revolution.

Publishes *The Practice and Theory of Bolshevism* in November.

1921   *The Analysis of Mind.*

In January, resigns from Trinity College due to tumultuous events in his personal life.

Russell, accompanied by his lover Dora Black, a British author, feminist, and socialist campaigner, visits Peking (now Beijing) to lecture on philosophy.

On August 26, returns to England. Dora is six months pregnant. Hastily divorces Alys Pearsall Smith and marries Dora Black on September 27.

On November 16, Dora gives birth to John Conrad Russell, 4th Earl Russell.

1922   *The Problem of China;* "Free Thought and Official Propaganda" (lecture).

Knowing he is extremely unlikely to be elected in

such a safe Conservative seat, unsuccessfully stands as a Labour Party candidate for Chelsea in the House of Commons.

1923   *The Prospects of Industrial Civilization* (with Dora Russell); *The ABC of Atoms.*

Again, unsuccessfully stands as a Labour Party candidate for Chelsea in the House of Commons.

Birth of daughter Katharine Jane Russell (later Lady Katharine Tait) on December 29.

1924   *Icarus; or, The Future of Science.*

1925   *The ABC of Relativity; What I Believe.*

1926   *On Education, Especially in Early Childhood.*

Delivers *Tarner Lectures* on the Philosophy of the Sciences at Trinity College.

1927   *The Analysis of Matter; An Outline of Philosophy;* "Why I Am Not a Christian."

Co-founds the Beacon Hill School with his wife Dora Black.

1928   *Sceptical Essays.*

1929   *Marriage and Morals,* in which he advocates for equality between the sexes, no-fault divorce, expanded sexual and professional freedom for women, and other progressive social measures.

1930   *The Conquest of Happiness.*

Daughter Harriet Ruth is born on July 8.

1931   *The Scientific Outlook.*

Older brother Frank dies, thus becomes 3rd Earl Russell.

1932   *Education and the Social Order.*

Separates from Dora, who, during their marriage, had two children with American journalist, Griffin Barry.

Awarded the De Morgan Medal.

Becomes Chair of the India League, the foremost lobby in the United Kingdom for Indian independence, a position he holds until 1939.

1934   *Freedom and Organization, 1814–1914.*

Awarded the Sylvester Medal.

1935   *In Praise of Idleness and Other Essays; Religion and Science.*

Divorce from Dora.

1936   *Which Way to Peace?*

On January 18, marries third wife, Oxford undergraduate Patricia ("Peter") Spence, who had been his children's governess since 1930.

1937   Birth of son with Patricia Spence, Conrad Sebastian Robert Russell, 5th Earl Russell, who would become a prominent historian and one of the leading figures in the Liberal Democrat party.

Returns to London School of Economics to lecture on the science of power.

Opposes rearmament against Nazi Germany.

1938   *Power: A New Social Analysis.*

Appointed visiting professor of philosophy at Chicago.

1939   Appointed professor of philosophy at the University of California at Los Angeles.

1940   *An Inquiry into Meaning and Truth.*

Changes position on war with Germany and advocates defeating Hitler, who he believes poses a permanent threat to democracy in Europe.

Appointed professor at City College of New York. He is quickly dismissed, however, after a court judgment pronounces him "morally unfit" to teach at the college because of his opinions.

1941   Appointed lecturer at the Barnes Foundation in Pennsylvania.

1942   Dismissed from Barnes Foundation, but wins a lawsuit against the Foundation for wrongful dismissal.

1943   Expresses support for the creation of an Israeli state; adopts a stance toward warfare called "relative political pacifism" that holds that war, in extreme circumstances, may be the lesser of two evils.

1944   Reappointed Fellow at Trinity College.

1945   *A History of Western Philosophy; The Bomb and Civilisation.*

1948   *Human Knowledge: Its Scope and Limits.*

Is one of twenty-four survivors (among a total of forty-three passengers) of an airplane crash in Hommelvik, Norway, in October.

"Authority and the Individual" (series of six BBC broadcasts).

In a public speech at Westminster School, addressing a gathering arranged by the New Commonwealth, Russell shocks some observers by suggesting that a preemptive nuclear strike on the Soviet Union might be justified.

1949   *Authority and the Individual.*

Awarded the Order of Merit; elected a Lifetime Fellow at Trinity College.

1950   *Unpopular Essays.*

Awarded the Nobel Prize in Literature.

1951   *New Hopes for a Changing World.*

1952   *The Impact of Science on Society.*

Patricia Spence divorces Russell. On December 12, marries Edith Finch, an American writer and biographer, whom he had known since 1925.

1953   *Satan in the Suburbs and Other Stories.*

1954   *Human Society in Ethics and Politics; Nightmares of Eminent Persons and Other Stories.*

Delivers "Man's Peril" address on the BBC on December 23.

1955   Enlists Albert Einstein and numerous other luminary scientists to sign the Russell-Einstein Manifesto, which is issued on July 9. It highlights the dangers posed by nuclear weapons and calls for world leaders to seek peaceful resolutions to international conflict.

1956   *Portraits from Memory and Other Essays.*

Expresses opposition to European imperialism in the Middle East.

1957   Elected president of the first Pugwash Conference on Science and World Affairs, which drew its inspiration from the Russell-Einstein Manifesto of 1955.

1958   *Understanding History and Other Essays; The Will to Doubt.*

Founds the Campaign for Nuclear Disarmament.

1959   *Common Sense and Nuclear Warfare; My Philosophical Development.*

1961   *Fact and Fiction; Has Man a Future?*

        At the age of eighty-nine, imprisoned for seven days for a "breach of the peace" after taking part in an anti-nuclear demonstration in London.

1963   *Essays in Skepticism; Unarmed Victory.*

        Awarded the inaugural Jerusalem Prize; establishes the Bertrand Russell Peace Foundation.

1966   *The ABC of Relativity.*

1967   Launches the International War Crimes Tribunal.

        Publishes *War Crimes in Vietnam* and a three-volume *Autobiography* beginning in 1967.

1970   On 31 January 1970, Russell issues a statement condemning "Israel's aggression in the Middle East," and in particular, Israeli bombing raids being carried out deep in Egyptian territory.

        On February 2, Bertrand Russell dies of influenza in Penrhyndeudraeth, Wales, United Kingdom. His body is cremated in Colwyn Bay on February 5. In accordance with his will, there is no religious ceremony but one minute's silence; his ashes are later scattered over the Welsh mountains.

Made in the USA
Coppell, TX
24 November 2024